WHO DO
YOU THINK
YOU ARE

tarcher perigee

An imprint of Penguin Random House LLC

penguinrandomhouse.com

First trade paperback edition 2019
Copyright © 2019 by Siobhán Gallagher

Most TarcherPerigee books are available at special quantity discounts for bulk purchase for sales promotions, premiums, fund-raising, and educational needs. Special books or book excerpts also can be created to fit specific needs. For details, write: SpecialMarkets@penguinrandomhouse.com.

ISBN 9780143130666

Printed in the United States of America
1 3 5 7 9 10 8 6 4 2
Book design by Siobhán Gallagher

WHO DO YOU THINK YOU ARE?

SIOBHÁN   GALLAGHER

A TarcherPerigee Book

ONE OF MY FAVORITE QUESTIONS TO ASK SOMEONE WHEN I'M FIRST GETTING TO KNOW THEM IS "WHO WERE YOU IN HIGH SCHOOL?" BECAUSE THAT WAS A TIME THAT WAS VERY INFORMED BY LABELS AND INVITES EMBARRASSMENT. TO ANSWER THIS, YOU NEED TO BE SELF-AWARE OF YOUR PAST AND PRESENT SELF AND CONSCIOUS OF WHAT SEPARATES THEN AND NOW.

IT CAN BE PRETTY CRINGEY REMEMBERING CERTAIN MOMENTS OF OUR YOUTH AND THE AWKWARDNESS THOSE YEARS INVOLVED, BUT THINKING OF PEOPLE AND MEMORIES FROM OUR PAST CAN HELP US UNDERSTAND WHO WE HAVE BECOME.

INDULGE IN THE NOSTALGIA CRINGE. JOG YOUR MEMORY, REFLECT ON WHO YOU WERE, AND APPRECIATE WHO YOU'VE BECOME!

DRAW A SELF-PORTRAIT

NAME: _____

AGE: _____

YEAR: _____

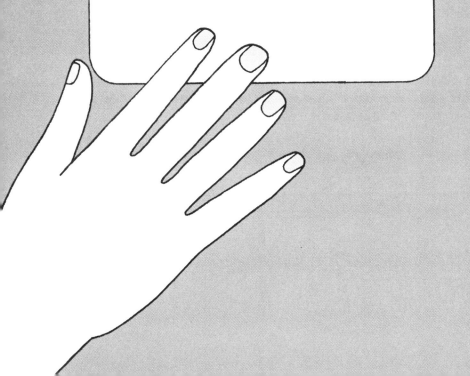

IF YOU COULD BOTTLE UP YOUR CHILDHOOD
WHAT WOULD IT SMELL LIKE?

GIVE YOUR 12-YEAR-OLD SELF ADVICE.

~~~~~~~~~~~~~~~~~~~~~~~~~~~~~~~~~~~~~~~

15-YEAR-OLD
SELF ~~~~~~~~~~~~~~~~~~~~~~~~~~~~~

20-
YEAR-OLD ~~~~~~~~~~~~~~~~~~~~~~~~~~~
SELF

YOURSELF TEN
YEARS FROM NOW

IMAGINE THERE IS A MUSEUM OF YOUR LIFE.
IN YOUR JOURNEY TO BECOME WHO YOU ARE, WHAT
MOMENT IS SO IMPORTANT THAT IT WOULD NEED A
LIFE-SIZE DIORAMA?

WRITE WHAT WOULD BE ON THE PLAQUE
IN FRONT OF THE DISPLAY.

IF YOU HAD TO CHANGE YOUR
MIDDLE NAME TO ANYTHING,
WHAT WOULD IT BE?
(AND YOU'RE NOT ALLOWED TO WRITE
YOUR CURRENT ONE, COME ON, PLAY ALONG.)

JAY

QUEEN

EARLY

DANGER

SKEETER

GUACAMOLE

DRAW YOUR CURRENT FAVORITE AT-HOME SLOB OUTFIT.

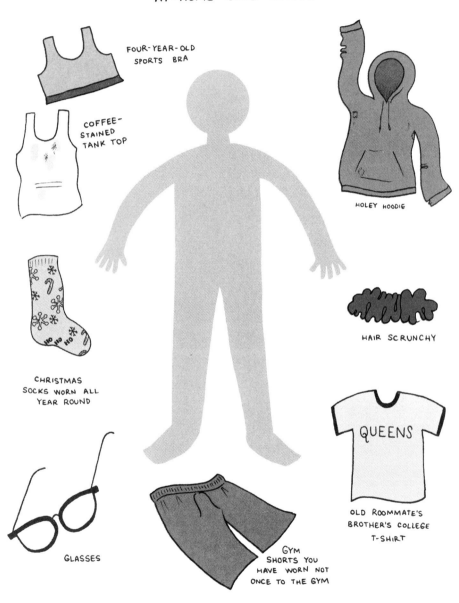

DRAW YOUR FAVORITE FEEL-GOOD OUTFIT
YOU HOPE YOU'D BE WEARING IF YOU RAN INTO AN EX.

SUNGLASSES

CALVIN KLEIN
SWEATER

THE HAT THEY
ALWAYS HATED

PURPLE
SKATER
DRESS

RED TANK TOP WITH
THE BUILT-IN BRA

A GROOVY
JUMPSUIT

THAT
LEATHER
SKIRT THAT
MAKES YOUR BUTT
LOOK <u>SO</u> GOOD

HIGHEST HEELS
YOU OWN

WHAT WERE YOUR LAST THREE GOOGLE SEARCHES? DO YOU THINK THESE ARE AN ACCURATE REPRESENTATION OF WHO YOU ARE?

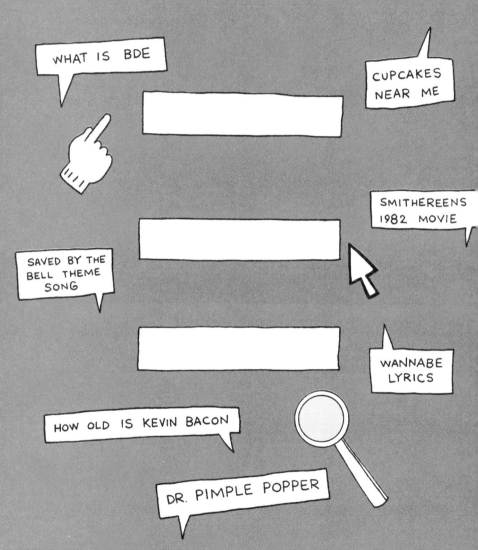

IF YOU WERE A CARTOON CHARACTER, WHAT WOULD YOUR UNIFORM BE? DRAW AND DESCRIBE THE CLOTHES CARTOON-YOU WOULD WEAR FOR THE REST OF THEIR TWO-DIMENSIONAL LIFE.

WHAT IS SOMETHING (OR SOMEONE)
YOU CAN'T BELIEVE YOU EVER LIKED?

CHUNKY
HIGHLIGHTS

OOF

VODKA

WHAT WAS I THINKING?

FRENCH
MANICURES

WARHEADS
CANDIES

YIKES

DANE
COOK

THAT GUY IN
SEVENTH GRADE
WHO TRIED TO
TATTOO HIMSELF

OVERPLUCKED
EYEBROWS

EW

MUSTARD-AND-
KETCHUP SANDWICHES

GROSS

CUT OUT WHICH LABELS APPLY
TO YOU AND KEEP THEM IN
YOUR POCKET.

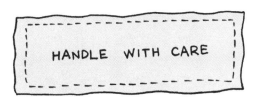

HANDLE WITH CARE

SENSITIVE

EXTREMELY INSENSITIVE

DELICATE

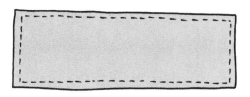

WHAT DID YOU DO ON YOUR
FAVORITE BIRTHDAY? HOW OLD WERE YOU?

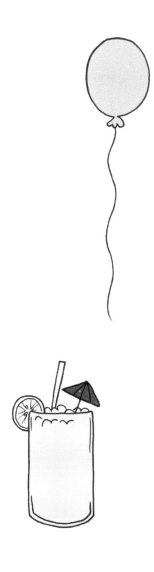

HOW WOULD YOU RATE
YOUR LIFE (SO FAR)?

1) ☹

2) UH, YEAH THIS SUCKS

3) UGH

4) MEH

5) WHATEVER

6) CAN'T COMPLAIN

7) COULD BE BETTER BUT
NOT BAD

8) LIKE AN EPISODE OF "THE OFFICE":
RELIABLE AND GREAT

9) OMG, LIKE SO GOOD. LIKE, YOU
DON'T EVEN KNOW.

10) I MUST HAVE AMAZING KARMA
FROM A PAST LIFE.

YOU'RE TEN. YOUR PARENTS GO OUT FOR THE NIGHT AND HIRE SOMEONE TO BABYSIT YOU. WHAT WOULD YOUR IDEAL BABYSITTER PLAN FOR YOU TO DO TOGETHER?

FILL IN YOUR IDEAL ACTIVITIES TO DO
AT THESE TIMES IN YOUR "PERFECT DAY."

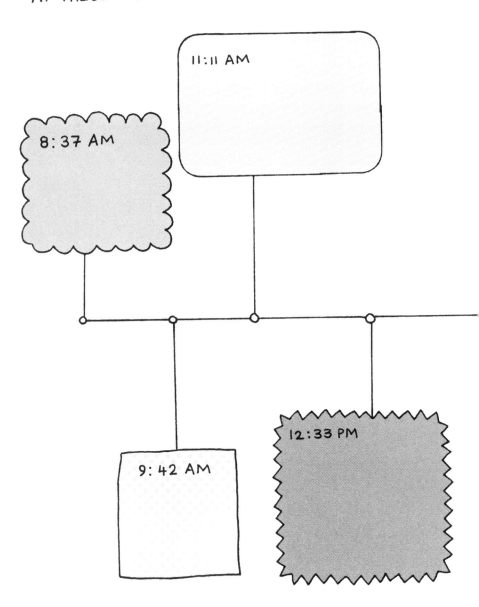

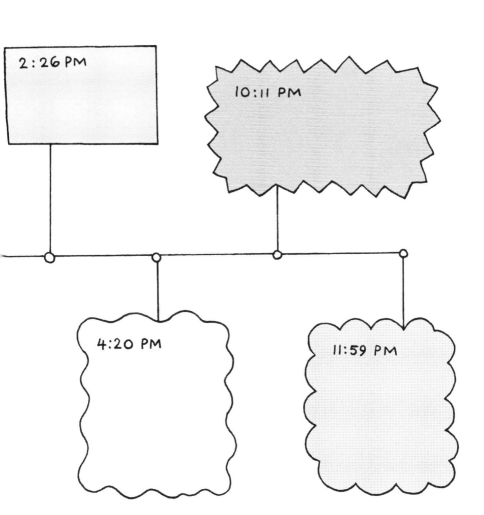

DRAW A BIRD'S-EYE VIEW OF YOURSELF
AND WRITE WHERE YOU ARE RIGHT NOW.

WHAT IS YOUR MOST EMBARRASSING CHILDHOOD MEMORY? IF YOU DON'T WANT TO DESCRIBE SPECIFICS, CIRCLE THE WORDS BELOW THAT APPLY.

SCHOOL   HOME   BATHROOM   TOILET

LOCKER   PUBLIC   ALONE   WET

KISS   BEDROOM   CLASSROOM   FAMILY

PEE   CRUSH   FART   EXCITED

CRY   VOMIT   LAUGH   FRIENDS

BOY   GIRL   HAIR   FALLING   HURT

DRAW OR WRITE YOUR FAVORITE
SNACKS FROM WHEN YOU WERE...

7 YEARS OLD

13 YEARS OLD

17 YEARS OLD

NOW

FILL OUT YOUR FAVORITES AT DIFFERENT AGES.

AGE	MOVIE	TV SHOW	CELEBRITY	HOBBY
6				
11				
15				
20				

COLLECT A FEW TCHOTCHKES FROM
YOUR CHILDHOOD OR THROUGH THE YEARS
AND KEEP THEM ON THE SAME SHELF
SO THEY DON'T GET LONELY.

FAVORITE TOY
FROM CHILDHOOD
FAMILY VACATION

CREEPY
ANTIQUE
DOLL FROM
LAST YEAR'S
ROAD TRIP

WOODEN
TOY WITH SECRET
COMPARTMENT FROM
8TH BIRTHDAY

WHITEST
SNEAKERS
AWARD

JOKE TROPHY
FROM WORK

LIST ALL THE PLACES YOU'VE BEEN TO
IN THE SHOES YOU'RE CURRENTLY WEARING.

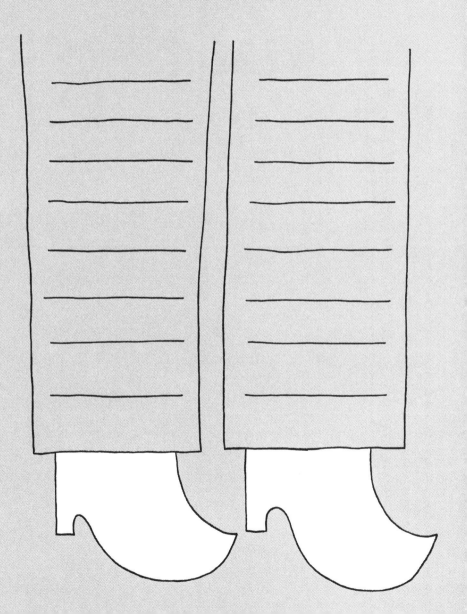

IF THE MOVIE OF YOUR LIFE WAS AT A VIDEO RENTAL STORE, HOW WOULD THE PLOT BE DESCRIBED ON THE BACK OF THE CASE?

YOUR STORY

WHAT'S A WORD OR PHRASE YOU THOUGHT MEANT ONE THING, ONLY TO DISCOVER YOU WERE WRONG WHEN YOU GOT OLDER?

GO ONLINE AND FIND A CLOSE FRIEND'S RECENT POST THAT THEIR PARENT COMMENTED ON. "LIKE" THE COMMENT (AND WRITE WHAT IT WAS AND WHOSE PARENT IT WAS HERE).

LIKE   REPLY

WHAT IS THE BEST MEMORY OF THE WORST JOB YOU'VE HAD?

GOOD TIPS

MET MONA

DISCOUNTED GROCERIES

RELAXING CAR RIDES

PIZZA FRIDAYS

FREE DONUTS

KEPT GLOVES FROM THE LOST & FOUND

I COULD READ ALL DAY

WHAT IS THE WORST MEMORY OF THE BEST JOB YOU'VE HAD?

LONG COMMUTE

WELL, I WORKED ALL WEEKEND.

MANIPULATIVE COWORKER

SPILLED COFFEE ON MONA'S KEYBOARD

THE GHOST

CRIED IN THE BATHROOM

FILING PAPERWORK

BEING STUCK IN THAT ELEVATOR FOR AN HOUR WITH GRANT

CREEPY BOSS

DON'T TALK TO ME BEFORE I'VE HAD MY COFFEE (OR AFTER).

LATE NIGHTS

HOW MANY TIMES DO I HAVE TO TELL YOU?

MARY YELLED AT ME

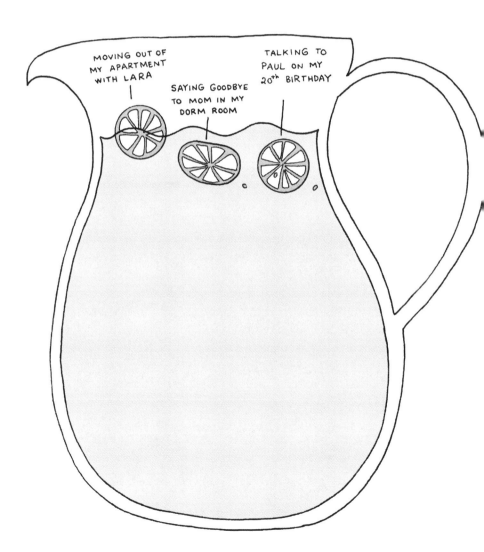

WHAT WAS YOUR FAVORITE THING TO DO WITH
FRIENDS ON A FRIDAY NIGHT WHEN YOU WERE
THIRTEEN? WHAT ABOUT NOW?

Then...

Now...

DRAW AND LABEL ALL THE THINGS
YOU'VE LOST THAT YOU WISH YOU'D FOUND.

HOME VIDEO

PHOTO BOOTH
PICTURE FROM
MICHELLE'S VISIT

OLD BAND SHIRT

MOM'S
RING

FAVORITE
DOLL

NEW
PURSE
DURING
TRIP TO
ITALY

HANDHELD
TOY

CUTE GIRL'S PHONE
NUMBER ON SCRAP PAPER

CALL ME
555
9244 Ali O

ARE YOU A MORNING PERSON OR NIGHT OWL?
DRAW YOUR FACE ON WHICH ONE APPLIES.

IF YOU COULD CHOOSE,
WHAT WOULD YOUR LAST MEAL BE?

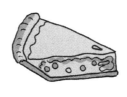

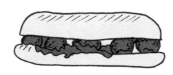

DO YOU HAVE ANY SCARS? WHERE?

WHAT MAGAZINE WOULD YOU BE INCLINED TO PICK UP AS A KID? NOW?

AGGGHH!

MONSTER MADNESS

- ☐ AS A KID
- ☐ NOW

flashy!

FUNKY FUN FASHION

- ☐ AS A KID
- ☐ NOW

EASY BREEZY

LAZY INDOOR FUN!

- ☐ AS A KID
- ☐ NOW

10011100101

COMPUTER DIGITAL STUFF!

BOOP BOOP BEEP BOOP

- ☐ AS A KID
- ☐ NOW

HUMMING & STRUMMING

-A MUSIC MAG-

- ☐ AS A KID
- ☐ NOW

BAKED

YUM!

fancy pastries

- ☐ AS A KID
- ☐ NOW

SMACKDOWN!

WRESTLING AT ITS BEST

- ☐ AS A KID
- ☐ NOW

SCORE!

GO TEAM GO!

SPORTS

- ☐ AS A KID
- ☐ NOW

GRR! MAG

CUTE MAMMALS!

CREEPY REPTILES!

- ☐ AS A KID
- ☐ NOW

BON VOYAGE!

EXPLORE WITH US!

- ☐ AS A KID
- ☐ NOW

PSS SST

celeb gossip!

- ☐ AS A KID
- ☐ NOW

SCRIBBLES

PUTTING the "ART" in "CARTOONS"!

- ☐ AS A KID
- ☐ NOW

IF YOU COULD TAKE A PILL THAT COULD ADD OR REMOVE A PERSONALITY TRAIT, WHAT WOULD THOSE TRAITS BE?

WRITE THE ONE THING IN YOUR LIFE YOU
WISH YOU COULD UNSEE (AND THEN COLOR
THESE SPECS INTO SUNGLASSES IF YOU
CAN'T STAND BEING REMINDED).

WHAT IS YOUR WORST BAD LITTLE HABIT?
IS IT OLD OR NEW?

BITING NAILS

ACCIDENTALLY SHARING OTHER PEOPLE'S SECRETS

BOREDOM SNACKING

CORRECTING OTHER PEOPLE'S GRAMMAR

ON PHONE TOO MUCH

MUMBLING

SUGARY DRINKS

JUST A LITTLE MESSY

RETAIL THERAPY

VIDEO GAMES

IF YOU COULD RELIVE ONE DAY OF YOUR LIFE,
WHAT DAY WOULD IT BE?

DECEMBER 25, 1990 LAST CHRISTMAS WITH MEG	MARCH 1, 2007 FIRST GALLERY SHOW	OCTOBER 20, 1982 MY SURPRISE PARTY	JUNE 13, 1995 PICNIC IN VICTORIA PARK	APRIL 22, 1978 MARRIED TONY
MAY 4, 2011 LUCY WAS BORN				JANUARY 2, 1991 BIRTH OF FIRST SON
DECEMBER 20, 1989 DAY BEFORE I WON THE LOTTERY				OCTOBER 14, 2000 RECEIVED AWARD FROM DEPARTMENT
SEPTEMBER 27, 2002 MET FRANCES				APRIL 11, 2006 FIRST TRIP TO EUROPE
MARCH 18, 1996 WORKING WITH MY FIRST BIG CLIENT				FEBRUARY 2, 1986 THE NIGHT OF SARA'S PARTY
APRIL 20, 2014 EXPLORING THE CITY WITH DIANE FOR THE FIRST TIME	JUNE 19, 1999 VISITING MATT FOR COMEDY MARATHON	MAY 26, 1975 WINNING THE FINALS	NOVEMBER 13, 2007 AMY WINEHOUSE SHOW	JULY 2, 1969 LISA SAID SHE LOVED ME FOR THE FIRST TIME

WHAT IS SOMETHING YOU'VE DONE THAT
YOU ARE MOST PROUD OF?

WHAT ITEM OF CLOTHING HAVE YOU HAD
THE LONGEST? KEEP IT AND NEVER THROW IT OUT.

FAVORITE
BASEBALL CAP

MOM'S COLLEGE
SHIRT

GRANDMOTHER'S
FUR COAT

HOODIE FROM
HIGH SCHOOL

SCREEN-PRINTED
TANK TOP

GRANDFATHER'S
CARDIGAN

ROLLING STONES
T-SHIRT FROM
HIGH SCHOOL

VINTAGE HEELS FROM
FRIEND'S SISTER

AS A KID, IF YOU WERE GIVEN $10, WHAT WERE
SOME THINGS YOU'D SPEND IT ON? WHAT WOULD
YOU DO WITH $10 IF YOU FOUND IT IN YOUR
POCKET NOW?

 Then...

 POKÉMON

Now...

IF YOU HAD TO GET A SINGLE TATTOO
TO BEST REPRESENT YOU, WHAT WOULD IT BE?

DO YOU REMEMBER YOUR
CHILDHOOD BEST FRIEND'S NAME?
THEIR BIRTHDAY?
THEIR HOME PHONE NUMBER?

WHAT WAS THE LAST TEXT YOU SENT AND RECEIVED?

Sent

Received

IF YOU HAD TO DESCRIBE YOUR 12-YEAR-OLD
SELF IN ONE WORD, WHAT WOULD IT BE?
WHAT ABOUT NOW?

Then...

Now...

WHAT ARE THE THINGS YOU DID OR LIKED
AS A KID THAT YOU NEVER QUITE GREW OUT OF?

WHAT ARE YOUR FAVORITE ASSOCIATIONS FOR EACH SEASON?
THAT INCLUDES SMELLS, MEMORIES, PLACES, PEOPLE, TASTES.

FALL

WINTER

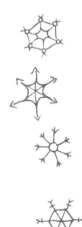

SPRING

SUMMER

FILL THIS TRASH CAN WITH THE NAMES OF
ALL THE PEOPLE WHO HAVE DONE YOU WRONG.

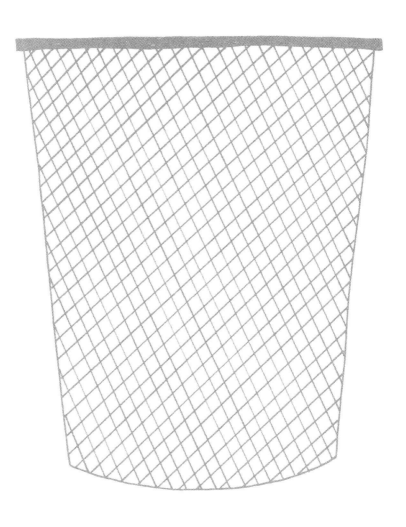

THEY SAY DON'T SWEAT THE SMALL STUFF
BUT YOU HAVE PERMISSION TO WHINE HERE. WHAT
LITTLE THINGS BUG THE S#@* OUT OF YOU?
DO YOU REMEMBER WHEN THEY FIRST ANNOYED YOU?

LOUD MOUTH-
BREATHERS

WHEN
YOUR
FRIEND
LISA
HASHTAGS
#HUBBY
IN HER
PHOTOS

PEOPLE
WHO MAKE
BAD JOKES
THEN STARE
EXPECTANTLY
AT YOU FOR
A LAUGH

... IT'S LIKE, Y'KNOW,
NOT EVERYONE'S IDEA OF,
Y'KNOW, FUN, BUT I THINK
IT'S GREAT, Y'KNOW?

MOLLY AT WORK WHO
SAYS "Y'KNOW" TOO MUCH

WERE YOU THE KIND OF KID WHO WOULD TALK IN THE CAR WHEN YOUR FRIENDS' PARENTS DROVE YOU HOME, OR WOULD YOU REMAIN QUIET UNTIL OUT OF THE PARENTS' PRESENCE?

HOW DID YOUR PARENTS MEET?
IF YOU DON'T KNOW, FIND OUT!

WHAT DID YOU HATE AS A KID THAT YOU REALLY TIED YOUR IDENTITY TO? HAS YOUR OPINION CHANGED?

I HATE BARNEY!

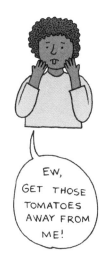

EW, GET THOSE TOMATOES AWAY FROM ME!

RED IS THE WORST COLOR!

WHAT IS YOUR FAVORITE 4 AM MEMORY?

DO YOU FEEL GUILTY ABOUT HOW YOU ONCE
TREATED SOMEONE? APOLOGIZE HERE AND
MAIL THIS PAGE TO THEM.

(OR TAKE A PICTURE AND SEND IT TO THEM.)

LAY ALL YOUR CARDS ON THE TABLE.
SHARE A FEW THINGS MOST PEOPLE DON'T KNOW ABOUT YOU.

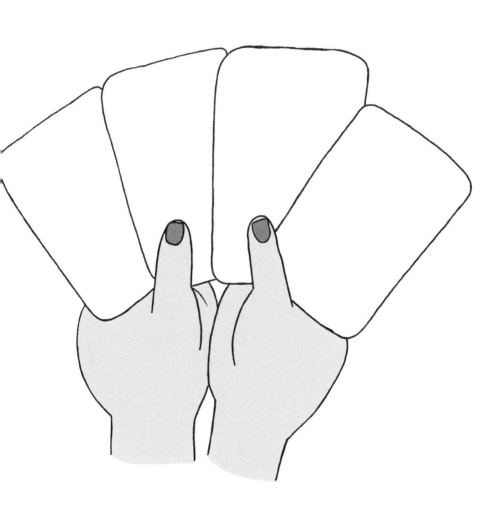

ARE YOU CARRYING BAGGAGE AROUND
FROM A PAST RELATIONSHIP? WRITE WHAT
YOU WISH YOU COULD TELL THEM AND FLIP THE
PAGE TO CLOSE THAT DOOR FOR GOOD.

WHERE DID YOU EXPECT TO BE AT YOUR CURRENT AGE WHEN YOU WERE A KID? DO YOU THINK YOU'D MAKE YOUR YOUNGER SELF PROUD?

WHO IN YOUR LIFE DO YOU HAVE THE MOST IMAGINARY CONVERSATIONS WITH IN YOUR HEAD?

DAD

THERAPIST

BUSINESS PARTNER

EX

BOSS

CURRENT GIRLFRIEND

BROTHER

MERYL STREEP

HUSBAND

FUTURE LOVER

FUTURE CHILDREN

UNCLE

OLD PROFESSOR

WHICH DO YOU PREFER?

LIGHT SWITCHES

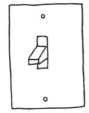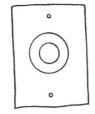

BATHROOM STALLS

FIRST
(CLOSEST
TO DOORS)

MIDDLE

LAST
(AGAINST
THE WALL)

EMAIL SIGN-OFFS

Thanks, Sam	Best, M	
THE THANKFUL	SHORT AND SIMPLE	NONE

WHAT IS AN UNUSUAL (OR BAD, FUNNY, OR EVEN BORING) HABIT YOU'VE HAD SINCE YOU WERE A KID?

I STILL LOVE PICKING SCABS!

AND YOU'RE GOING OUT LIKE THAT?

TEASING OTHERS

HOLDING YOUR BREATH WHEN PASSING A CEMETERY

LICKING THE FLAVORING OFF CHIPS BEFORE EATING THEM

CHEWING THE ENDS OF PENCILS

NOW LET'S SEE WHAT WE HAVE HERE...

TALKING TO YOURSELF

1. FOLD EACH CORNER TO OPPOSITE CORNER WITH PAPER FACEDOWN

2. FOLD ALL CORNERS TO THE CENTER

3. TURN YOUR PAPER OVER SO THE FOLDED SIDE IS FACEDOWN

4. JUST LIKE IN STEP 2, FOLD ALL CORNERS TO THE CENTER

5. YOUR PAPER SHOULD NOW LOOK LIKE THIS

6. NOW FOLD IT IN HALF SO YOUR FINGERS CAN TUCK INTO THE BOTTOM

7. READY TO PLAY!

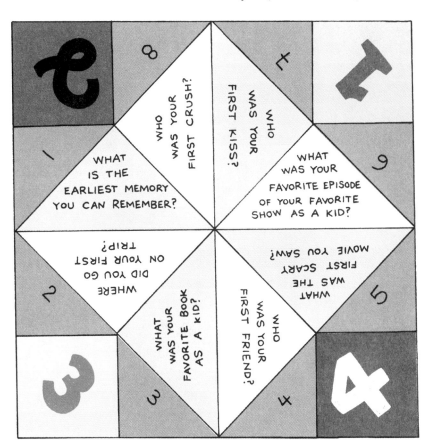

WHO WAS YOUR FIRST CRUSH?

WHO WAS YOUR FIRST KISS?

WHAT IS THE EARLIEST MEMORY YOU CAN REMEMBER?

WHAT WAS YOUR FAVORITE EPISODE OF YOUR FAVORITE SHOW AS A KID?

WHERE DID YOU GO ON YOUR FIRST TRIP?

WHAT WAS THE FIRST SCARY MOVIE YOU SAW?

WHAT WAS YOUR FAVORITE BOOK AS A KID?

WHO WAS YOUR FIRST FRIEND?

IS THERE A RECURRING PLACE THAT
APPEARS IN YOUR DREAMS? DESCRIBE IT
IN WORDS OR PICTURES.

CHILDHOOD HOME

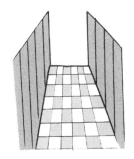

HIGH SCHOOL
HALLWAY

A CREEPY
FOREST

AN IMAGINARY PLACE

Then...

Now...

DO YOU REMEMBER THE DATE OF YOUR FIRST KISS?

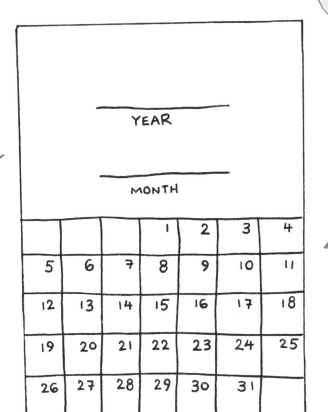

YEAR

MONTH

			1	2	3	4
5	6	7	8	9	10	11
12	13	14	15	16	17	18
19	20	21	22	23	24	25
26	27	28	29	30	31	

CHECK OFF WHICH INGREDIENTS WOULD
BE NEEDED IN THE RECIPE TO MAKE "YOU."

RECIPE

- [ ] 2 tsp OF INSECURITY
- [ ] 1 cup OF APPRECIATION OF GOOD PUNS
- [ ] 1 DOLLOP OF AMBITION
- [ ] 2 tbsp OF GUILT
- [ ] A DASH OF ANGER ISSUES
- [ ] 1 cup OF SERIOUSNESS
- [ ] 1 cup OF SILLINESS
- [ ] WHIPPED SASS
- [ ] _____
- [ ] _____
- [ ] _____
- [ ] _____
- [ ] _____

WRITE THE ADVICE YOU'D GIVE TO YOUR YOUNGER SELF. TEAR THIS PAGE OUT AND SLIP IT INTO A BOOK AT YOUR LOCAL BOOKSTORE.

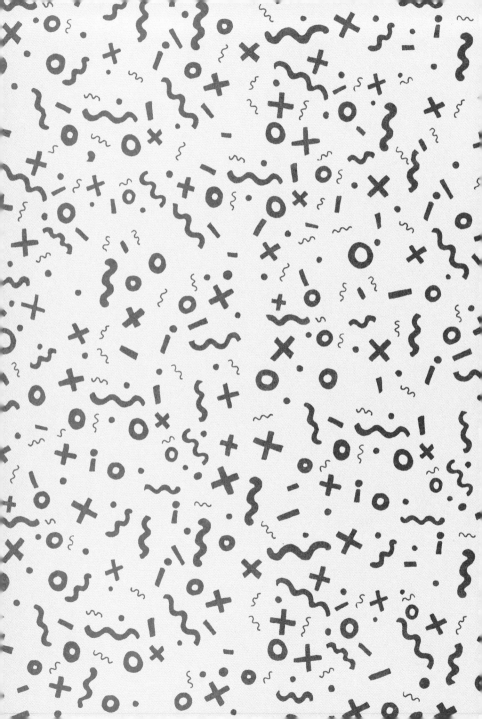

WHAT WAS YOUR FAVORITE SUBJECT IN MIDDLE SCHOOL? WHAT ABOUT IN HIGH SCHOOL?

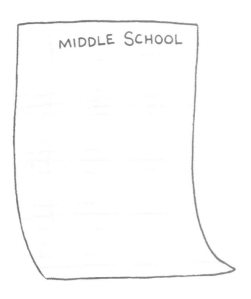

MIDDLE SCHOOL

HIGH SCHOOL

DO YOU REMEMBER WHAT YOUR
SIGNATURE LOOKED LIKE TEN YEARS AGO?
TRY TO RECREATE HERE.

~~~~~~~~~~~~~~~~~~~~~~~~~

OLD SIGNATURE

~~~~~~~~~~~~~~~~~~~~~~~~~

CURRENT SIGNATURE

WHAT WAS YOUR BEST FRIEND'S NAME AT...

WHAT WAS YOUR BIGGEST INSECURITY GROWING UP?
WHAT IS YOUR BIGGEST INSECURITY NOW?

Then...

Now...

IF YOU WERE TRAPPED ON A DESSERT
ISLAND (YES, YOU READ THAT RIGHT), WHAT ONE
SWEET FOOD WOULD YOU WANT?

DRAW AND LABEL THE FLOOR PLAN OF YOUR
CHILDHOOD BEDROOM.

WHAT KIND OF KID WERE YOU IN HIGH SCHOOL?
CIRCLE THE STEREOTYPES THAT APPLY

DRAMA KID

ATHLETE

LONER

PUNK

POPULAR

NERD

A.P. STUDENT

TOUGH STUFF

PRINCESS

ART KID

TEACHER'S PET

WHO WERE YOU?

WHAT DO YOU NORMALLY CARRY IN
YOUR POCKETS OR BAG? CIRCLE ALL
THAT APPLY AND FILL IN YOUR OWN.

CARDS

KEYS

OLD RECEIPTS

LIPSTICK

LONE... UH...
RAISIN?

MATCHBOOK
FROM BAR

GROSS EMERGENCY
MINT

A BOOK

PEN THAT HAS A 50% CHANCE OF WORKING

OLD
TISSUES

USELESS,
GOOD-FOR-NOTHING
PENNIES

SUSIE MEYERSON
Personal Management
(212) 555-5656

SOMEONE'S OLD
BUSINESS CARD YOU
FEEL BAD FOR
TOSSING

A SEEMINGLY ENDLESS
COLLECTION OF BOBBY PINS

WHAT IS YOUR LEAST FAVORITE PHRASE TO HEAR FROM A STRANGER? WRITE IT HERE, TEAR IT OUT, CRUMPLE IT UP, AND TOSS IT ACROSS THE ROOM.

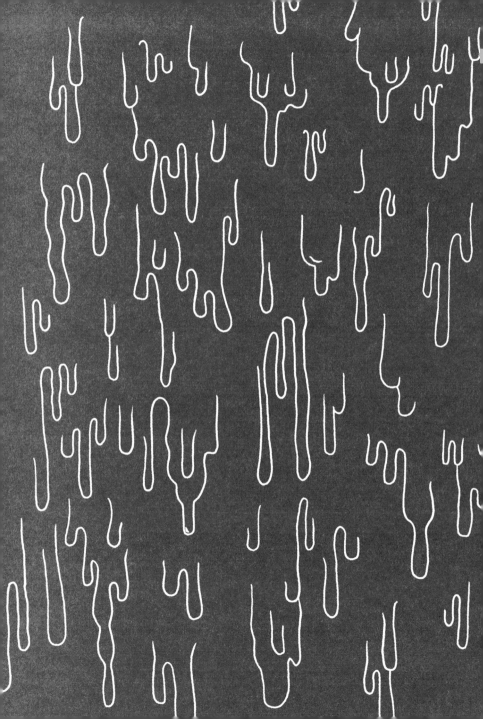

HIDE WHAT YOU'RE MOST ASHAMED OF HERE:

IF YOUR LIFE WAS A MOVIE, WHAT WOULD THE TITLE BE? WHO WOULD YOU CAST TO PLAY YOURSELF?

DONALD GLOVER

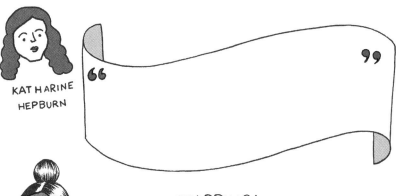

STARRING:

KATHARINE HEPBURN

MINDY KALING

TIFFANY HADDISH

GROVER

BRUNETTE TONI COLLETTE

MICHAEL CERA

JOHN CHO

ZOE LISTER-JONES

NICK KROLL

WHAT TASKS ARE YOU CURRENTLY PUTTING OFF?
WRITE THEM HERE AND FEEL GOOD THAT AT LEAST NOW
YOU'VE GOT A TO-DO LIST.

• PICK UP LAUNDRY • CLEAN BASEMENT • GO TO DMV •

SOCIOLOGY HOMEWORK • DROP OFF CLOTHES TO SHELTER DOWNTOWN

• FIX BIKE • MAIL CHECKS • APPLY FOR JOBS • BUY STAMPS •

REPLY TO EMAILS • PATCH UP COAT POCKET HOLES • BACK UP LAPTOP

WRITE WHICH PARENT YOU RESEMBLE MOST
IN THESE CATEGORIES:

PHYSICALLY:

SENSE of HUMOR:

PERSONALITY:

SOCIALLY:

FOOD PREFERENCES:

TEMPERAMENT:

MUSIC TASTE:

WHAT WAS YOUR IDEA OF FUN AS A KID?
WHAT DID YOU PLAY?

PILING UP MATTRESSES AND PLAYING "CASTLE"

YEAH, USE THE KETCHUP AS BLOOD!

MAKING "MOVIES" WITH DAD'S CAMCORDER

TRUTH OR DARE

I DARE YOU TO... LICK THE FLOOR!

SETTING TOYS ON FIRE

SCRABBLE

FREEZE TAG

JUMPED ON PILLOWS AND PRETENDED THE FLOOR WAS LAVA

TONY HAWK "RO SKATER" N PLAYSTATION

PRETENDED TO BE CATS AND POKÉMON

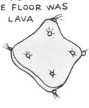

AS A KID, WHAT DID YOU WANT
TO BE WHEN YOU GREW UP?

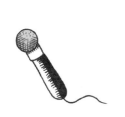

I WISH I WAS LIKE ANGELICA'S MOM FROM "RUGRATS"

IF YOU APPEARED ON THE FRONT PAGE OF THE PAPER, WHAT WOULD YOUR IDEAL HEADLINE SAY?

The Cool Dork Times

APOCALYPSE POSTPONED!

COOL DOG HAVING A GREAT DAY

IF YOU DIED TOMORROW, WHAT WOULD AN HONEST VERSION OF YOUR TOMBSTONE SAY?

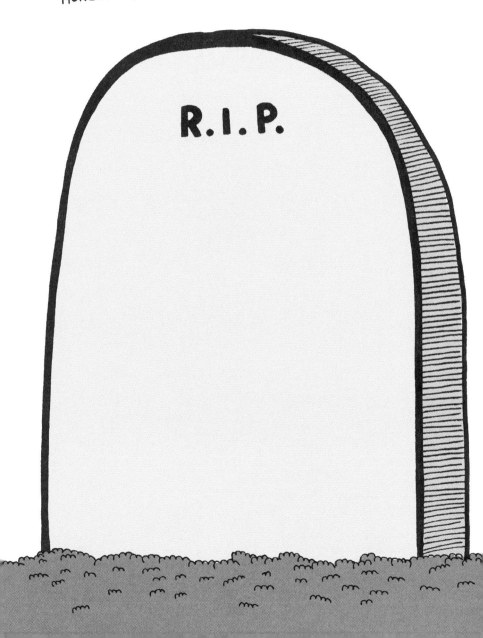

WHAT SONG PLAYS FROM THE SOUNDTRACK OF YOUR LIFE WHEN...

YOU'RE GETTING READY IN THE MORNING:

_____

YOU'RE ON YOUR WAY TO A PARTY:

_____

YOU'RE EXCITED ABOUT SOMETHING NO ONE YOU KNOW CARES ABOUT:

_____

YOU'RE TRAVELING:

_____

YOU'RE PISSED OFF AT SOMEONE:

_____

YOU'VE HAD A GOOD DAY:

_____

YOU'RE LONELY:

_____

WHAT FICTIONAL CHARACTER (IN MOVIES, TV SHOWS, BOOKS, ANYTHING) DO YOU IDENTIFY WITH MOST?

MICHAEL SCOTT ("THE OFFICE")

THE DUDE ("THE BIG LEBOWSKI")

MARIE ("WHEN HARRY MET SALLY")

RALPHIE ("A CHRISTMAS STORY")

BOJACK HORSEMAN

PEGGY ("MAD MEN")

ELAINE ("SEINFELD")

CHRIS KRAUS ("I LOVE DICK")

TAMMY ("ELECTION")

MAX ("RUSHMORE")

REBECCA ("CRAZY EX-GIRLFRIEND")

JOEL ("ETERNAL SUNSHINE OF THE SPOTLESS MIND")

BILL HAVERCHUCK ("FREAKS AND GEEKS")

LISA SIMPSON ("THE SIMPSONS")

IF YOU HAVE SIBLINGS, WRITE YOUR NAMES
FROM OLDEST TO YOUNGEST. WHAT DO YOU BOND
OVER THE MOST WITH EACH?

WHAT IS A FRUSTRATING MEMORY FROM YOUR CHILDHOOD?

WHAT IS SOMETHING FRUSTRATING THAT HAPPENED
TO YOU RECENTLY?

FILL IN THE BLANKS:

WHAT MADE YOU FIRST REALIZE YOU WERE IN LOVE WITH SOMEONE?

YEAR: _____

HOW/WHO: _____

_____

_____

WHEN WAS THE FIRST TIME YOU WERE DUMPED?

YEAR: _____

HOW/WHO: _____

_____

_____

WHAT WAS A REASON YOU BROKE UP WITH SOMEONE?

YEAR: _____

HOW/WHO: _____

_____

_____

_____

WHAT SONGS WOULD YOU INCLUDE ON
YOUR IDEAL ROAD TRIP PLAYLIST?

LOVE
SHACK

I SAW THE SIGN

1. _____

2. _____

3. _____

4. _____

WHERE THE
STREETS HAVE
NO NAME

5. _____

6. _____

7. _____

8. _____

9. _____

10. _____

TOTO

AFRICA

ROAD TO NOWHERE

WHAT WAS YOUR
FAVORITE CHILDHOOD SNACK?

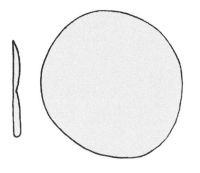

WHAT IS YOUR
FAVORITE COMFORT
FOOD NOW?

WHAT WAS A TYPICAL
DINNER AS A KID?

WHAT IS A TYPICAL
DINNER FOR YOU NOW?

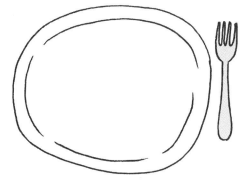

WHAT KEEPS YOU UP AT NIGHT?

CHECK ALL THAT APPLY.

- ☐ BOY TROUBLE
- ☐ GIRL TROUBLE
- ☐ EXISTENTIAL DREAD
- ☐ WORK
- ☐ FAMILY
- ☐ KIDS
- ☐ MICE
- ☐ A PREDICTION A WITCH WARNED YOU ABOUT
- ☐ MOVIE PLOT HOLES
- ☐ THE GOVERNMENT
- ☐ RELYING ON OTHERS
- ☐ FINDING AN APARTMENT
- ☐ HEALTH
- ☐ DOG'S HEALTH
- ☐ INTERNET DOG'S HEALTH
- ☐ HOW RAMONA RESPONDED TO BETHENNY ON LAST NIGHT'S "REAL HOUSEWIVES"
- ☐ GLOBAL WARMING
- ☐
- ☐
- ☐
- ☐
- ☐
- ☐
- ☐
- ☐

WHAT KIND OF PEOPLE DO YOU
GET ALONG WITH BEST? DESCRIBE
WHAT YOU USUALLY LOOK FOR IN FRIENDS.

TO WHOM DO YOU OWE THE MOST IN YOUR LIFE?
WRITE AS MANY PEOPLE AS YOU WANT
AND HOW THEY HAVE HELPED YOU.

SET A TIMER FOR FIVE MINUTES AND USE THAT
TIME TO WRITE DOWN EVERYTHING YOU CAN REMEMBER FROM
YOUR ADOLESCENCE AND CHILDHOOD. THIS CAN BE A COMPLETE
STREAM-OF-CONSCIOUSNESS RAMBLING OF EMOTIONS, PEOPLE,
AND EVENTS FROM YOUR EARLY YEARS.

FOLLOW THE TRAIN

WRITE ALL YOUR DISLIKES
(SMALL OR BIG):

GETTING GLASSES
FOGGED UP

A LONG STRAND
OF SWEAT DRIPPING
DOWN MY BACK

THE FEELING
OF SCRATCHING
VELVET AND
CORDUROY

WEIRD
SPORTS FAN
RIVALRIES

IT'S BY
ACCIDENT!
IT'S IN LINE!

CILANTRO

WHEN PEOPLE SAY
"ON ACCIDENT" OR
"ON LINE"

SITTING BESIDE
A STRANGER AND
HAVING THEIR ARM
LIGHTLY TICKLING
MY ARM

WHEN DOGS ARE FORCED TO
WEAR OUTFITS THEY HATE

WRITE ALL YOUR LIKES
(BIG OR SMALL):

DOGS GETTING
THEIR BEDS READY

WATERMELON-
FLAVORED CANDIES
(BUT NOT THE FRUIT
THEMSELVES)

WHEN ELLEN
DEGENERES CRY-
LAUGHS

OLDER LADIES
CALLING ME TERMS
OF ENDEARMENT

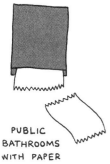

PUBLIC
BATHROOMS
WITH PAPER
TOWELS INSTEAD
OF AIR DRYING

AL HIRSCHFELD'S
HIDDEN NINAS

HOLIDAY TWINKLY LIGHTS

WHAT WAS A FORK-IN-THE-ROAD MOMENT
IN YOUR LIFE THAT INFLUENCED WHERE YOU ARE NOW?

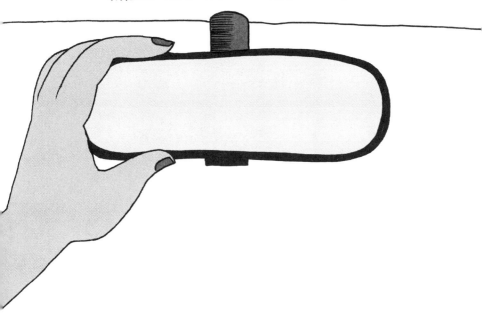

WHO AND WHERE DO YOU HOPE TO BE IN TEN YEARS?

SIOBHÁN GALLAGHER IS AN ILLUSTRATOR
AND BOOK DESIGNER LIVING IN NEW YORK CITY.
HER ILLUSTRATIONS HAVE BEEN FEATURED IN
PUBLICATIONS SUCH AS *THE NEW YORK TIMES*, *ELLE
CANADA*, *US WEEKLY*, *THE HUFFINGTON POST*, AND *THE
NEW YORKER*. SHE SELF-PUBLISHES MULTIPLE ZINES
PER YEAR, DRAWS EVERY DAY, AND IS IN A
CONSTANT STATE OF NOSTALGIA.
THIS IS HER SECOND BOOK.